outlining your NOVEL

WORKBOOK

Step-by-Step Exercises for Planning Your Best Book

outlining your NOVEL

WORKBOOK

Step-by-Step Exercises for Planning Your Best Book

K.M. WEILAND

SCOTTSBLUFF, NEBRASKA

Outlining Your Novel Workbook: Step-by-Step Exercises for Planning Your Best Book
Copyright © 2014
K.M. Weiland

Cover design by Damonza.

Graphics in Chapters 1-5 by The Codeville.
Graphic in Chapter 6 by Matt Gemmell.

Published by PenForASword Publishing.

Printed in the United States of America.

ISBN: 978-0-9857804-2-5

Also by K.M. Weiland:

Outlining Your Novel: Map Your Way to Success

Structuring Your Novel: Essential Keys for Writing an Outstanding Story

Structuring Your Novel Workbook: Hands-On Help for Building Strong and Successful Stories

Jane Eyre: The Writer's Digest Annotated Classic

Conquering Writer's Block and Summoning Inspiration

Fiction

A Man Called Outlaw

Behold the Dawn

Dreamlander

Digital Shorts

The Memory Lights

One More Ride in the Rain

The Saddle Daddy Rode

TABLE OF CONTENTS

INTRODUCTION

WHAT *IS* AN outline? Is it a road map? A battle plan? A checklist?

It's all three—and more. As I discuss in *Outlining Your Novel: Map Your Way to Success*, the outline can be anything you want it to be. You can fill up three notebooks with story plans, or you can scribble a couple thoughts on some Post-It Notes and call it good. How an outline manifests isn't important. The only thing that matters is that your outline helps you figure out this great big puzzle we call a novel.

WHY OUTLINES MAKE NOVEL WRITING EASIER

On the surface, novels seem simple enough. A beginning, a middle, an end. Throw in a couple characters, a heroic quest, an epic romance—and *voila!* A story is born.

True enough. But if you're one of those people who's tried throwing all those ingredients into a bowl, mixing them up, and letting them bake, you already know the recipe isn't foolproof. In fact, that simple little recipe you *thought* would make a perfect story? Turns out it barely covers the essential ingredients.

Novels aren't like boxed mac and cheese. Boiling water and stirring in Velveeta just isn't enough to produce a masterpiece. Novels are more like pasta parmigiana—made from scratch. Sure, there's some magic and some luck involved. But there's also a lot of science.

In short, *there's a lot to remember*. In all honesty, there's more to remember than most of us can handle while in the white-hot rush of writing a first draft. If we dash in there, throwing about flour and eggs, hoping we've got it all right without bothering to check Nonna's recipe, then we're going to *need* magic and luck.

But if we prepare beforehand, with an outline, we'll be able to assemble all the ingredients, heat the oven to the right temperature, and approach our dough and sauce with the confidence of foreknowledge.

Stories, for all their seeming simplicity, are complicated. They're puzzles, in which all the pieces have to fit just so. They're not random dreamscapes that tumble out of our brains, fully formed. Rather, they're cohesive wholes, in which the beginning and the end must be planned as a partnership. If we don't know how a story is going to end, we'll never know how to properly begin it. If we don't know the elements that will play into the story, we won't know how to build a framework to support them.

And that is where the outline comes in.

The outline allows us to see the big picture before we have to start fitting together the tiny, detailed pieces. As a result, we're able to write our first drafts with confidence and purpose and save ourselves hours of revision.

HOW TO USE THIS WORKBOOK

When *Outlining Your Novel: Map Your Way to Success* came out in 2011, I was overwhelmed by writers' hunger for information on outlining. Most authors recognize the need to bring cohesion to the complicated art form of the novel via some kind of planning. But many are hung up on the old notion that outlines have to be Roman numeraled lists.

Outlining Your Novel presented an actionable approach to planning stories from the ground up—creating a premise, brainstorming plot ideas, interviewing characters, and plotting story arc. The method I shared in the book is the one I've developed in writing my own historical and speculative novels. But it is endlessly adaptable to the specific needs of each writer.

What you will find in the pages of this workbook is a complete (and, often, expanded) list of every question and every step I describe in *Outlining Your Novel*. Each chapter offers an introduction to the concepts discussed in the exercises, as well as examples from popular books and movies and my own outlines. I have also included a page-number guide to help you locate the associated chapters in *Outlining Your Novel*. I recommend you start by reading that book—just as you would a textbook—before embarking on the workbook. You will understand the principles and their applicability better in context.

Each chapter of the workbook builds upon the next, in a series of steps that will help you move from your story's big picture to the smaller details and back again. The more thorough you are in responding to each question and filling in each blank, the more prepared you will be to write your novel. But don't hesitate to skip around. Some of the sections (such as those on foreshadowing and settings) can't be completed until you've finished all the other steps. Remember: what you're trying to create here is *your* best process. If you feel constrained by any of the questions or feel they don't apply to your story, go ahead and skip them.

Your outline may require more space than what is provided for your responses here. Before you begin the exercises, grab a notebook so you can migrate your note-taking should you need more space.

Outlines can transform your writing process into a practicable and focused story-crafting machine. But don't settle for any ol' kind of outline. Use the exercises in the following pages to dig deep into the heart of your story and take full advantage of your outline's storytelling power.

1
PREMISE

B Y THE TIME you sit down to outline, your story idea will probably have been chasing around in your head for anywhere from several days to several years. You may not know much about your story yet, but you know enough to start. You probably have ideas for several main characters, a handful of scenes, a general conflict, and maybe a broad sense of the ending.

Your first goal is to hammer all this down into a premise: one or two sentences that convey the characters, the plot, and the theme. Who is your hero? What does he want? Who or what is keeping him from getting what he wants? What's at stake if he doesn't get it? The premise is where you discover and solidify these decisions.

This is your mission statement for your book. This is where you figure out not just *what* story you want to write, but what *kind* of story you want to write. Fast-paced action thriller? Leisurely generational saga? Epic historical romance?

The premise you create now won't be written in stone. If you come up with better ideas down the line, don't hesitate to rewrite your premise sentence. But for now distilling preexisting ideas of your story into a compact sentence or two (which you'll learn about in detail in a few pages) will help you understand where you'll need to go next in your outline.

THE "WHAT IF" QUESTION

ALL STORIES BEGIN with a concept (a battle in space, two people falling in love, a dog getting lost), and most concepts begin with a "what if" question. Even when the question isn't articulated, every novel, every story, and every article is ultimately inspired by those words.

Ask yourself every "what if" question that pops to mind regarding your story. Some of your ideas will be ridiculous; most will probably never make it into your book. But don't censor yourself. By allowing yourself to write down every idea, no matter how crazy, you may come up with story-transforming gems.

Once you've selected the few ideas that might work, start looking for tangents: "If such and such happened, then *what if* this also happened? Or *what if* this happened instead?" The possibilities are endless. Be sure to return to this section and add to your list whenever a new idea strikes.

(For more information on the "what if" question, see pages 48-49 in *Outlining Your Novel.*)

EXAMPLES:

- **"What if a little boy's brain grew too quickly for his body to keep up?"**
  (*Ender's Shadow* by Orson Scott Card)

- **"What if an orphan were given a fortune by an unknown benefactor?"**
  (*Great Expectations* by Charles Dickens)

- **"What if children were forced to fight in gladiatorial games?"**
  (*The Hunger Games* by Suzanne Collins)

What if _two teachers at the same school were interested in eachother_?

What if _only one teacher was interested_?

What if _they couldn't get the timing right_?

What if _one threatened sexual harassment charges due to brokenheart_?

What if _he tries his hand at online dating_?

What if __she worries about the failed aftermath__ ?

What if __she is afraid of her unfulfilled dreams__ ?

What if __they don't end up together__ ?

What if __he/she date student's parents__ ?

What if __jealousy takes hold of one of them__ ?

What if __they are incompatible__ ?

What if __drama from exes springs up__ ?

What if __they are soulmates__ ?

What if __one of the secondary characters tries to get with her__ ?

What if __the pursuer becomes the pursuee__ ?

What if __they can't get the timing right__ ?

What if __their students get involved advocating the relationship__ ?

What if __everyone gets involved advocating the relationship__ ?

What if __rejection leads to a period of self-discovery__ ?

What if __antagonist has issues causing her to be incapable of receiving love__ ?

What if __it is just infatuation and not true eros__ ?

What if __they see eachother out of context of work__ ?

What if _____ ?

WHAT IS EXPECTED?

A VARIATION OF the "what if" question is "What is expected?" In the first column, list everything you can imagine the average reader expecting to happen in your type of story. Across from each item, write an alternate event. Put a check beside any idea you *want* to fulfill.

(For more information on the "What Is Expected?" question, see pages 49-50 of *Outlining Your Novel*.)

EXAMPLES:

It is expected the hero will get the girl. ☑   The hero doesn't get the girl. ☐

It is expected the bad guy will die. ☐   The bad guy doesn't die. ☑

It is expected they will end up together ☑   they wont end up together ☐

It is expected they will have outside support ☐   there will be outside antagonism ☑

It is expected for tommy issues ☑   love right away ☐

It is expected love at first sight ☐   enduring building of love ☑

It is expected no unhappiness ☐   there will be broken hearts ☑

It is expected to affect career ☑   career before love ☐

It is expected _____ ☐   _____ ☐

It is expected _____ ☐   _____ ☐

It is expected _____ ☐   _____ ☐

It is expected _____ ☐   _____ ☐

It is expected _____ ☐   _____ ☐

WHAT IS UNEXPECTED?

FLIP THE PREVIOUS exercise on its head and brainstorm concepts readers would not automatically expect from your story, based on its genre, its characters, and early plot. Put a check beside any idea that sounds promising.

(For more information on the "What Is Unexpected?" question, see page 50 in *Outlining Your Novel.*)

EXAMPLES:

- **It is unexpected the hero will lose his superhuman powers.**
  (*Spider-Man 2* directed by Sam Raimi)

- **It is unexpected that opponents in a crucial contest will fall in love.**
  (*The Night Circus* by Erin Morgenstern)

- **It is unexpected a teenage girl will set out on the trail to avenge her father's murder.**
  (*True Grit* by Charles Portis)

It is unexpected that _threat of legal action_ ☑

It is unexpected that _work past problems_ ☑

It is unexpected that _there will be forgiveness in love_ ☑

It is unexpected that _there will be patience in love_ ☑

It is unexpected that _there will be heartbreak_ ☑

It is unexpected that _there will be true love_ ☑

It is unexpected that _____ ☐

It is unexpected that _____ ☐

It is unexpected that _____ ☐

It is unexpected that _____ ☐

It is unexpected that _____ ☐

It is unexpected that _____ ☐

It is unexpected that _____ ☐

It is unexpected that _____ ☐

It is unexpected that _____ ☐

It is unexpected that _____ ☐

It is unexpected that _____ ☐

It is unexpected that _____ ☐

It is unexpected that _____ ☐

It is unexpected that _____ ☐

It is unexpected that _____ ☐

It is unexpected that _____ ☐

It is unexpected that _____ ☐

It is unexpected that _____ ☐

It is unexpected that _____ ☐

It is unexpected that _____ ☐

It is unexpected that _____ ☐

THE TWO-SENTENCE PREMISE

WHAT IF" QUESTIONS are powerful. But if we don't refine them into premise sentences, we're not taking full advantage of them. Crafting a good premise sentence helps you identify viable ideas and solidify your conflict, character, and plot. In one sentence (or two, if you have just too many goodies to cram into one), you should be able to discover all your story's salient facts.

Start by answering the following questions. If you don't currently know the answer to any question, skip it and keep going. Return to fill in the blanks after you've figured out more of your story. There is no right order in which to do any of this.

(For more on the premise sentence, see pages 50-52 in *Outlining Your Novel*.)

EXAMPLES:

- Orphaned gypsy Heathcliff (**protagonist**) grows up to love (**objective**) his adopted sister Cathy (**situation**), but when Cathy (**opponent**) marries her wealthy neighbor (**disaster**), Heathcliff sets in motion a terrible vengeance that will pit him against everyone he knows (**conflict**).
(*Wuthering Heights* by Emily Brontë)

- Restless farm boy (**situation**) Luke Skywalker (**protagonist**) wants nothing more than to leave home and become a starfighter pilot, so he can live up to his mysterious father (**objective**). But when his aunt and uncle are murdered (**disaster**) after purchasing renegade droids, Luke must free the droids' beautiful owner and discover a way to stop (**conflict**) the evil Empire (**opponent**) and its apocalyptic Death Star.
(*Star Wars: A New Hope* directed by George Lucas)

Who is your **protagonist**? _Lyle Ellam_ .

Is your protagonist ordinary or extraordinary? _ordinary_ .

What is his **situation** at the beginning of the story? _wayward bachelor_ .

What is the protagonist's personal condition at the beginning? _lonely and lovelorn; ready to start the next great chapter of his life_

How is it going to be changed, for better or worse, by the protagonist himself or by the antagonistic force? _he will grow and become a we instead of an I_.

Is your protagonist's situation ordinary or extraordinary? _ordinary_.

What is the protagonist's **objective**? _to find and fall in love_.

Who or what is the main **opponent**? _Holly Stargle (object of his affection)_

What early **disaster** will befall the protagonist and force him out of his "normal world" and into the main conflict? _he will fall into deep unrelenting infatuation_

What **conflict** will result from the hero's reaction to the disaster? _not romantically or emotionally available_.

What is the logical flow of cause and effect that will allow this conflict to continue throughout the story? _mis-timing of emotional availability_
.

Is this idea **plausible**? _ostensibly so_.

Is this idea **original**? _in execution it is_.

How is this idea different from similar stories? _the notion of sacrifice makes it unique_.

How can you strengthen its originality _the fast-pace heartbreak and retaliatory nature_.

What is the **focus** of your story? _love_ .

    What will be its genre? _humorous romance/personal growth_ .

    Who will be its intended audience? _young adult romance seekers_ .

Using the information you've discovered in answering the above questions, put them all together into a premise sentence.

Your premise sentence(s): _Newly appointed advanced placement highschool teacher Lyle Ellam has set his sights upon the Arts teacher Holly Stoyle. Tragically and completely emotionally unavailable, Mr. Ellam must search for a cure to his love lorn elsewhere while his true feelings bring him nothing but trouble._

PROTAGONIST
A likeable, relatable,
or interesting lead
character.

CONFLICT
The larger, story-wide
conflict the protagonist
must enter after the disaster.

SITUATION
The character's problems
and limitations, defined
by his "Normal World."

What Makes
a Good
Story Premise?

DISASTER
An event that forces the
protagonist to leave the
Normal World of the First Act.

OBJECTIVE
The protagonist's story
goal (separate from his
life goal or scene goal).

OPPONENT
The person (or thing)
standing in the way
of the protagonist's goal.

LOG LINE

NOTHER VERSION OF the premise sentence is the log line. Used in the movie industry to hook potential directors and producers, the log line forces authors to distill the essence of their stories. Doing so not only helps you focus your early conception of a story, it also reveals core strengths (or weaknesses). Fill in the blanks in the following log-line templates, then ask yourself, "Based on this one sentence, is this a story I would be interested in reading?" How can you make the story even *more* interesting?

If your story seems to have more than one main character, write a log line for each character. Which seems to best encapsulate the main thrust of the plot? This character is almost certainly your protagonist.

(For more information on log lines, see *Finding the Core of Your Story* by Jordan Smith.)

EXAMPLES:

- An idealistic (**descriptor**) lawyer (**protagonist**) must bring law and order to the uncivilized American West (**do something**) even if it means a duel (**climactic encounter**) with a psychotic (**descriptor**) gunslinger (**antagonist**).
  (*The Man Who Shot Liberty Valance* directed by John Ford)

- After he is discovered unconscious and wounded in the ocean (**something happens**), an amnesiac (**descriptor**) assassin (**protagonist**) must track down his missing past (**do something**) and set a trap (**set up**) in order to gain his freedom (**climactic encounter**) from his black ops (**descriptor**) handlers (**antagonist**).
  (*The Bourne Identity* directed by Doug Liman)

LOG LINE TEMPLATE #1:

A __handsome__ __teacher__ must __find love__
    descriptor   protagonist   do something

that will __disarm a sheltered woman__ and __result in a relationship__
        set up   climactic encounter

with a __doubtful__ __artist__ .
    descriptor   antagonist

LOG LINE TEMPLATE #2:

After _**transferring schools**_ to _**NYCMHS**_,
        something happens   set things up

a _**handsome**_ _**teacher**_ must _**find love**_
   descriptor   protagonist   do something

that will _**disarm a gaurded artist**_ and _**establish a relationship**_
              set up   climactic encounter

with a _**beautiful**_ _**artist**_.
       descriptor   antagonist

STORY SUMMARY

USING THE INFORMATION you've already discovered, expand your premise sentence or log line into a full-fledged summary. If you don't yet know what happens in your story, feel free to make it up as you go along. Pretend you're writing the back cover copy for the finished novel. Start with a hook, introduce your protagonist, and explain what he wants and what conflict is standing in his way. Hint at the stakes in the final battle. Aim for no more than three hundred words.

EXAMPLES:

- After her brother dies in a trauma room, nurse Claire Avery can no longer face the ER. She's determined to make a fresh start—new hospital, new career in nursing education—move forward, no turning back. But her plans fall apart when she's called to offer stress counseling for medical staff after a heartbreaking daycare center explosion. Worse, she's forced back to the ER, where she clashes with Logan Caldwell, a doctor who believes touchy-feely counseling is a waste of time. He demands his staff be as tough as he is. Yet he finds himself drawn to this nurse educator . . . who just might teach him the true meaning of healing.
(*Critical Care* by Candace Calvert)

- Given the chance to train as a squire, kitchen servant Achan Cham hopes to pull himself out of his pitiful life and become a Kingsguard Knight. When Achan's owner learns of his training, he forces Achan to spar with the Crown Prince—more of a death sentence than an honor. Meanwhile, strange voices in Achan's head cause him to fear he's going mad. While escorting the prince to a council presentation, their convoy is attacked. Achan is wounded and arrested, but escapes from prison—only to discover a secret about himself he never believed possible.
(*By Darkness Hid* by Jill Williamson)

Your story summary: _After receiving his numerous advanced degrees Lyle Ellam will begin his career at an elite NYC_

high school as an advanced placement teacher.
He becomes immediately ensconsed with romantic
feelings of a talented artist and teacher. She is tragically
and completely unavailable and emotionally damaged. After
threat of torture Lyle braves the storm to win the
heart of Holly Stople. With significcant sacrifice
Lyle proves his feelings and shows his trustworthiness.

Pre-Outline Questions

BEFORE YOU DIG any deeper into your outline, now is the time to take a long, hard look at your premise. Are you milking it for everything it's worth? If you can identify possible weaknesses and create new strengths now, before you even begin plotting your story, you'll be able to take full advantage of your premise and save yourself work in the long run. To help you analyze your premise, answer the following questions.

Again, it's great if you brainstorm answers to these questions upfront. But if you don't yet know the answers, feel free to leave the questions blank and return to them later when you've discovered a little more about your story.

(For more information about pre-outline questions and taking full advantage of your premise, see pages 52-55 in *Outlining Your Novel*.)

Can you name five big moments that will occur in the plot and think of four complications for each of these moments?

Big Moment #1: _____.

Complication #1: _____.

How will this complication make your protagonist uncomfortable?_____

_____.

What additional settings will this complication require?_____

_____.

Complication #2: _____.

How will this complication make your protagonist uncomfortable?_____

_____.

What additional settings will this complication require? _____

_____.

Complication #3: _____.

How will this complication make your protagonist uncomfortable?_____

_____.

What additional settings will this complication require?_____

_____.

Complication #4: _____.

How will this complication make your protagonist uncomfortable?_____

_____.

What additional settings will this complication require? _____

_____.

Big Moment #2: _____.

Complication #1: _____.

How will this complication make your protagonist uncomfortable?_____

_____.

What additional settings will this complication require? _____

_____.

Complication #2: _____.

How will this complication make your protagonist uncomfortable? _____

_____.

What additional settings will this complication require?_____

_____.

Complication #3: _____.

How will this complication make your protagonist uncomfortable? _____

_____.

What additional settings will this complication require?_____

_____.

Complication #4: _____.

How will this complication make your protagonist uncomfortable?_____

_____.

What additional settings will this complication require? _____

_____.

Big Moment #3: _____.

Complication #1: _____.

    How will this complication make your protagonist uncomfortable?_____

    _____.

    What additional settings will this complication require? _____

    _____.

Complication #2: _____.

    How will this complication make your protagonist uncomfortable?_____

    _____.

    What additional settings will this complication require?_____

    _____.

Complication #3: _____.

    How will this complication make your protagonist uncomfortable?_____

    _____.

    What additional settings will this complication require?_____

    _____.

Complication #4: _____.

    How will this complication make your protagonist uncomfortable?_____

    _____.

    What additional settings will this complication require? _____

    _____.

Big Moment #4: _____.

Complication #1: _____.

    How will this complication make your protagonist uncomfortable?_____

    _____.

    What additional settings will this complication require?_____

    _____.

Complication #2: _____.

    How will this complication make your protagonist uncomfortable?_____

    _____.

    What additional settings will this complication require?_____

    _____.

Complication #3: _____.

How will this complication make your protagonist uncomfortable?_____

_____.

What additional settings will this complication require?_____

_____.

Complication #4: _____.

How will this complication make your protagonist uncomfortable?_____

_____.

What additional settings will this complication require?_____

_____.

Big Moment #5: _____.

Complication #1: _____.

How will this complication make your protagonist uncomfortable?_____

_____.

What additional settings will this complication require?_____

_____.

Complication #2: _____.

    How will this complication make your protagonist uncomfortable?_____

    _____.

    What additional settings will this complication require?_____

    _____.

Complication #3: _____.

    How will this complication make your protagonist uncomfortable?_____

    _____.

    What additional settings will this complication require?_____

    _____.

Complication #4: _____.

    How will this complication make your protagonist uncomfortable?_____

    _____.

    What additional settings will this complication require?_____

    _____.

Which character will be affected most by the inciting event? _____.

    Is this character your protagonist? _____.

Name two major problems or anxieties in this character's life:

Problem #1: _____.

How does this problem affect other characters?_____

_____.

Problem #2: _____.

How does this problem affect other characters?_____

_____.

Which problem offers the most potential for conflict and drama? _____

_____

Who is your main antagonist? _____.

Is your main antagonist a conscious entity? _____.

If so, what is his motive? _____.

What is his goal? _____.

What are his values? _____.

Name two minor antagonists:

Minitagonist #1: _____.

What is his motive? _____.

What are his values? _____.

Minitagonist #2: _____.

    What is his motive? _____.

    What are his values? _____.

How will these antagonists each attack your protagonist's weakness in different ways?

    Main Antagonist: _____.

    Minitagonist #1: _____.

    Minitagonist #2: _____.

How will these characters stand between your protagonist and what he wants?

    Main Antagonist: _____.

    Minitagonist #1: _____.

    Minitagonist #2: _____.

How will the minor antagonists oppose the main antagonist?

    Minitagonist #1: _____.

    Minitagonist #2: _____.

How will the minor antagonists oppose each other? _____

_____.

CREATIVE EXERCISE:

For each of the following basic premises, brainstorm three unexpected twists that will take full advantage of the premise's potential and add originality.

- A starship captain's military convoy is hijacked.
- A young boy and his friend are kidnapped by outlaws.
- A princess accepts an arranged marriage in order to spy on a rival kingdom.

SOMETHING TO THINK ABOUT:

1. Why are you interested in outlining?
2. What are your favorite brainstorming techniques?
3. What do you believe is the single most important factor in discovering originality?
4. Do you think there is any advantage to stories that feature ordinary characters in extraordinary settings versus extraordinary characters in ordinary settings?
5. Before you wrote your premise sentence, were you already familiar with how the required elements would manifest in your story—or did you discover them as you wrote?
6. Was summarizing your story into one or two sentences an easy place from which to start your outline, or did you find it difficult?

RESOURCES:

- "How to Write a Novel: The Snowflake Method," Randy Ingermanson, helpingwritersbecomeauthors.com/OYNW-Ingermanson
- "Writing a Novel Scene by Scene," Debbie Roome, helpingwritersbecome authors.com/OYNW-Roome
- *The Anatomy of Story*, John Truby, Chapter 2
- *Writing the Breakout Novel*, Donald Maass, Chapter 2
- *Techniques of the Selling Writer*, Dwight V. Swain, Chapter 5

2
GENERAL SKETCHES

EXPLORATION IN AN outline takes a tiny percentage of the time it would take in a first draft—and with half the mess. In an outline, you never have to delete fifty pages of work just because you failed to realize an idea was headed down a dead-end alley. In an outline, you can explore all those interesting possibilities, discover which ones work and which ones don't, and enter your first draft equipped to write a solid and scintillating story.

The meat of your outline will begin with your "general sketches." You won't be plotting every detail of your novel just yet. Right now, you're slitting the packing tape and opening the box that holds your story. You're discovering the beautiful and disparate parts inside that box and learning how they fit together.

In many ways, this is the most important stage of the outline, since this is where you give yourself permission to throw every idea—no matter how offbeat—onto the page. You'll be writing down what you already know about the story, crafting it into a synopsis of sorts, and discovering the plot holes. Take the time to ask yourself lots of "what ifs" and "whys." Why is the character behaving this way? Why is she bitter about her past? What if he makes a radically different decision at a crucial point in the plot?

THE SCENE LIST

BY THE TIME you're ready to start outlining, you will probably have several basic ideas for characters and a handful of scenes in which you can see them interacting. Start by making a list of the scenes you already have in your head. Some of the events you write down may actually end up happening *before* the beginning of your book, but, at this point in the outline, you shouldn't worry about shaping the format of the story or choosing the best place to begin the first chapter. Right now, you're just getting all your thoughts on paper.

The important thing isn't to create new scenes or try to fill in the blanks in the plot. All you need to do at this stage is dig through your imagination for every single idea you've ever come up with in relation to this story. Not all of them will work; some will be downright silly. But because all of them were conceived more or less organically and have had time to grow to maturity in the warmth of your imagination, every single one is worth writing down.

When you reach a part of the story that doesn't make sense or needs to be fleshed out, write yourself a quick note and move on. These blank areas are the secret tunnels that will lead you to adventures unknown. When you've finished your scene list, go back over what you've written and use the highlighting guide, below, to color code your ideas for easier organization.

(For more information on the scene list, see pages 62-64 in *Outlining Your Novel*.)

Color-Coding Guide
Blue = Complete Idea That Needs No Further Fleshing Out
Green = Incomplete Idea That Needs More Brainstorming
Yellow = Good Idea That Will Influence Further Brainstorming
Pink = Idea That Needs to Be Moved Earlier or Later in the Scene Sequence
Orange = Good Ideas That Don't Directly Influence Plot (e.g., setting details)

EXAMPLES:

- **Marcus Annan, a disillusioned professional soldier, is wounded during the Third Crusade and captured by Saracens. He is nursed back to health by a Scotswoman who had accompanied her doomed husband to the War and was herself captured by the Muslims.**

Annan, once recovered, is given the opportunity to escape. Feeling a debt of gratitude to the Lady Mairead, he offers to aid her escape. For some important reason, they marry, with the intention of separating once in France or England.

They escape and are met by Annan's indentured servant Peregrine Marek. They keep their marriage a secret from him.

Annan has an enemy, for some reason. Can't remember his name, so we'll just call him Sir Enemy. They are at odds over something.
(*Behold the Dawn*)

- •1. Chris dreams of a woman who warns him to stay in his world and then shoots him.
  2. Chris receives strange letters warning him to "stay away from the shrink."
  3. Chris learns he visits a parallel world when he sleeps.
  4. Chris wakes up in Lael in the middle of a battle.
  (*Dreamlander*)

What scenes do you already know about?

_____

_____

_____

_____

_____

_____

_____

_____

_____

_____

_____

_____

_____

_____

_____

_____

_____

_____

_____

_____

_____

_____

_____

_____

_____

_____

_____

_____

_____.

If you haven't exhausted your ideas, feel free to continue in a notebook or on the computer.

CONNECTING THE DOTS

ONCE YOU HAVE completed your scene list and color coded your ideas, go back and look for all the green highlights that indicate questions or incomplete ideas. List each below (try to phrase each as a question, even if that's not how you originally wrote it in the scene list), then brainstorm solutions to each problem.

(For more information on connecting the dots, see pages 63-69 in *Outlining Your Novel*.)

EXAMPLES:

Question: Who is Annan's enemy? And why?
Answer: Maybe Annan's enemy is a bishop or something. Annan could have left the Church because of indifference, of course, but that's too dispassionate for his character. He could have left because he saw through the hypocrisy of the bishop. No, better, I think, that he left because he was hurt—maybe a friend was killed unjustly by the bishop.

Question: _____

_____.

Answer: _____

_____

_____

_____

_____.

Question: _____

_____.

Answer: _____

_____

_____

_____

_____

_____.

Question: _____

_____.

Answer: _____

_____

_____

_____

_____

_____.

Question:_____

_____.

Answer:_____

_____

_____

_____

_____.

Question:_____

_____.

Answer: _____

_____

_____

_____

_____.

Question: _____

_____.

Answer: _____

_____

_____

_____

_____

_____.

Question: _____

_____.

Answer: _____

_____

_____

_____

_____.

If you haven't finished answering all the questions you raised in the scene list, feel free to continue in a notebook or on the computer. When you've finished, go back through your answers and highlight in green any new questions you may have raised. Repeat this exercise by posing and answering each of those questions. Repeat as often as necessary, until you've filled all the obvious plot holes and created a logical sequence of events.

CHARACTER ARC AND THEME

AS YOUR OUTLINE begins to take shape, it's important to keep in mind several key factors in your character's arc: motive, desire, goal, conflict, and theme. The earlier you can identify these things and ensure your plot is capable of properly incorporating them, the easier your job will be in the long run. Every so often, take a mental step back from the creative whirlwind you're scribbling and evaluate these elements. Sometimes these things can be easy to overlook as you're summarizing your plot, but the last thing you want to do is spend months on your outline only to start writing your first draft and discover you're missing a key element. Get a head start on story problems by answering the following questions.

(For more information on character arcs, see pages 75-80 in *Outlining Your Novel*.)

What is the Thing Your Character Wants? _____

_____.

This is the foundation for the story goal your character is trying to accomplish. This is his outer need, the thing he knows he wants and thinks he must accomplish to reach his primary objective.

EXAMPLES:

- **Jane Eyre wants to marry her soul mate, Rochester.**
  (*Jane Eyre* by Charlotte Brontë)
- **Rick Blaine wants to reunite with his lost love Ilsa.**
  (*Casablanca* directed by Michael Curtiz)

Why does your character want this (i.e., what's his motive)? _____

_____.

What is he doing to try to obtain it (i.e., how is he putting his goal into action)? _____

_____.

How can you frustrate his desires and goals to create conflict? _____

_____.

What is the Thing Your Character Needs? _____

_____.

This need is curled up deep inside your character and is at the core of the weakness holding him back from achieving his full potential. Sometimes, this need can stand in stark contrast to the want (previous page), to the point that achieving either one means completely abandoning the other. However, sometimes, this need can end up being the perfect complement to the want—in which case, it's the character's resistance to this need that stands in the way of his achieving not just its fulfillment, but the fulfillment of the want as well.

Examples:

- Jane's need to remain true to her moral duty (as well as her need to grow into the strength to truly stand as Rochester's equal) impedes her from remaining with Rochester after she learns of his insane wife.

- Rick's need to fight the Nazis and support Ilsa's freedom-fighter husband prevents him from running away with Ilsa.

objectives as sources of conflict

How do these two desires conflict with one another? _____

_____.

What Lie does your character believe that is keeping him from the Thing He Needs,

prompting him to believe he *must* gain the Thing He Wants? _____

_____.

What Truth does your protagonist need to discover? _____

_____.

What weakness or flaw is central to your character's life as a result of his belief in the Lie?

_____.

How are people in his life being hurt by this weakness? _____

_____.

Who is your character in the beginning of the story? _____

_____.

    What does he care about? _____

    _____.

    What does he believe in? _____

    _____.

    How can you show the character's imperfection/incompleteness in the beginning?

    _____.

How will your character have changed by the middle of the story? _____

_____.

    What scenes will you use to demonstrate how he has evolved? _____

    _____.

    What scenes will you use to demonstrate he is still imperfect/incomplete? __

    _____.

Who will your character be in the end of your story? _____

_____.

    What will be your character's "moment of revelation" in the climax? _____

    _____.

How will you prove the character's inner change to readers? _____

_____.

What "tools" (mentor's advice/untenable situations/new mindsets, etc.) will

your character require to improve himself? _____

_____.

How will your character behave in various situations?

characters behave differently for different audiences and social contexts

With his parents? _____.

With his love interest? _____.

At work? _____.

When being mugged? _____.

When relaxing? _____.

Write a list of each of your prominent characters' goals and the motive for each.

EXAMPLES:

- Annan wants to die on the battlefield because he feels the guilt for his crimes is too great a burden to go on carrying.
- Mairead wants to find Matthias of Claidmore because Gethin the Baptist told her Matthias would save her.
- Marek wants to finish his term of indentureship to Annan because Maid Dolly is waiting for him back in Scotland.

1. _____ wants to _____, because s/he

_____.

2. _____ wants to _____, because s/he

_____.

3. _____ wants to _____, because s/he

_____.

4. _____ wants to _____, because s/he

_____.

5. _____ wants to _____, because s/he

_____.

6. _____ wants to _____, because s/he

_____.

7. _____ wants to _____, because s/he

_____.

8. _____ wants to _____, because s/he

_____.

9. _____ wants to _____, because s/he

_____.

10. _____ wants to _____, because s/he

_____.

How can your supporting characters' beliefs about the central thematic principle reflect or contrast your protagonist's belief in the Lie?

1. What does the antagonist believe? _____

   _____.

2. What does the sidekick believe? _____

   _____.

3. What does the love interest believe? _____

   _____.

4. What does the mentor believe? _____

   _____.

CONFLICT

ONCE YOU HAVE your character's motive, desire, and goal in place, you can start creating obstacles between him and his goals. Conflict fuels fiction, and frustration fuels conflict. Every time the characters (and the readers) begin to think victory and happiness are around the bend, you have to find some way to circumvent them. Whatever your chosen genre, frustration is the key to keeping characters and readers on their toes. If you're going to give readers what they want, you have to deny your characters what *they* want. Start by writing a list of the ten worst things that could happen to your character.

(For more information on conflict, see pages 80-86 of *Outlining Your Novel*.)

EXAMPLES:

- **Get separated from your owner in a strange gas station.**
(*Toy Story* directed by John Lasseter)

- **Get dumped by your soul mate without explanation.**
(*Sense & Sensibility* by Jane Austen)

- **Have your escape tunnel come up twenty yards short of safety in the woods.**
(*The Great Escape* directed by John Sturges)

1. _____.

2. _____.

3. _____.

4. _____.

5. _____.

6. _____.

7. _____.

8. _____.

9. _____.

10. _____.

What will keep your protagonist and/or your antagonist from walking away from the conflict? Put a check next to whichever of the following "adhesives" are keeping them together. Explain how.

EXAMPLES:

- **Survival:** Sanger Rainsford is forced to hunt down and kill his insane antagonist, a Russian aristocrat, before the aristocrat kills him. ("The Most Dangerous Game" by Richard Connell)

- **Love:** Mr. Darcy can't forget about Elizabeth, even after she explicitly turns down his proposal of marriage. (*Pride & Prejudice* by Jane Austen)

- **Enjoyment/Obsession:** The Joker pursues Batman out of obsessive enjoyment of their cat-and-mouse game. (*The Dark Knight* directed by Christopher Nolan)

☐ Duty/Obligation.

    How?_____.

☐ Hatred/Vengeance.

    How?_____.

☐ Survival.

    How?_____.

☑ Love.

    How? loves her as a mother_____.

☐ Enjoyment/Obsession.

    How?_____.

☐ Greed.

    How?_____.

☑ Pride.

    How?_____.

☐ Other.

    How?_____.

Write at least one way in which each of the following supporting characters can hinder (or seem to hinder) your protagonist's pursuit of his goal, in even a small way.

    Love interest: _____.

    Sidekick: _____.

    Mentor: _____.

List five unexpected situations into which your protagonist's pursuit of his goal might lead him:

    1. _____.

    2. _____.

    3. _____.

    4. _____.

    5. _____.

What is the estimated timeline for your story? (Use the calendar on page 127, if necessary.)

How many:

__3__ Years

_____ Months

_____ Days

_____ Hours

Would you be able to raise the stakes if you shortened the timeline? Why?

possibly, in part though I had one of the
novels set in lunar and seasonal cycles.

3 years is also better for movie
adaptations

CREATIVE EXERCISE:

Watch one of your favorite movies or read one of your favorite books. Can you identify the theme? How is this theme presented through the subtext? Is it ever stated outright? *Love, bravery, do not fear death ⟹ HP*

SOMETHING TO THINK ABOUT:

1. Did you already have quite a few scenes you knew you would want to include in your story? Did you change your mind about any of them as you wrote them down?
2. Was discovering your protagonist's motive easier or more difficult than discovering your antagonist's motive?
3. Do you experience a physical sensation (such as shortness of breath) when you come up with a good idea?
4. Do you find that free writing encourages or discourages your creativity?
5. Have you ever written a character you despised? If so, do you think your feelings about him helped or hindered you in writing him?

RESOURCES:

- "How Minor Characters Help You Discover Theme," K.M. Weiland, helpingwritersbecomeauthors.com/2014/01/minor-characters-help-discover-theme
- "How the Antagonist Affects Character Arc," K.M. Weiland, helpingwritersbecomeauthors.com/2013/12/antagonist-affects-character-arc
- "Tips for Creating Thematic Resonance," K.M. Weiland, helpingwritersbecomeauthors.com/2011/11/posts-8
- "How to Explore Your Character's Motivations," Joe Bunting, helpingwritersbecomeauthors.com/OYNW-Bunting
- "Conflict vs. Tension," Writers Helping Writers, helpingwritersbecomeauthors.com/OYNW-Puglisi

HOW MUCH TIME DO STORIES NEED?

LENGTH OF BOOK

THE GREAT GATSBY — **180 PAGES**

PRIDE AND PREJUDICE — **256 PAGES**

THE LORD OF THE FLIES — **272 PAGES**

THE HUNGER GAMES — **384 PAGES**

ENDER'S GAME — **384 PAGES**

JANE EYRE — **624 PAGES**

TIMELINE OF BOOK

THE GREAT GATSBY **5 MONTHS, 23 DAYS**

PRIDE AND PREJUDICE **1 YEAR, 10 DAYS**

THE LORD OF THE FLIES **5 MONTHS, 4 DAYS**

THE HUNGER GAMES **27 DAYS**

ENDER'S GAME **5 YEARS, 7 MONTHS**

JANE EYRE **9 YEARS, 5 MONTHS, 3 WEEKS**

helpingwritersbecomeauthors.com

3
CHARACTER SKETCHES: BACKSTORY

N OW THAT YOUR General Sketches have helped you understand your plot progression and story arc, and now that you've filled in the obvious plot holes, it's time to work on Character Sketches—beginning with backstory.

By this point in the outlining process, you should have a basic idea of the major plot points. You know who your heroes are, you know what they're after, and you know some of the things they must accomplish to reach their goals. But your concept of who they are and what, in their individual pasts, has shaped them into the people you need them to be, may still be foggy.

Before you can tell others your story, you have to tell yourself its prequel. The key to crafting stories with many layers—stories with depth and ballast—is to never ignore the blank spaces in your characters. Don't let them get away with telling you only what they must to make the story work. Search out the shadows in their pasts, discover their parents, their childhood friends, their catalysts. Don't just accept that your main character is a cop; find out *why* he became a cop. Don't just slap a scar on your heroine; discover *where* the scar came from.

THE INCITING AND KEY EVENTS

WHERE DO YOU start your backstory? The obvious answer is "at the beginning": *Where was your character born? Who were his parents? What events in his childhood shaped his outlook?* But sometimes a less intuitive method will prove more effective in bringing clarity and focus to discovering your character's backstory. Instead of starting at the beginning, try starting at the moment when the backstory officially ends and the story itself begins: the inciting event.

The inciting event is the moment that forever changes your character's world. It knocks over the first domino in the line of dominoes that form your plot. It sets off an irrevocable chain reaction that will eventually lead your character to the maelstrom of your climax. This event shapes your character's existence throughout your book. This is the event your backstory must logically lead up to. By beginning with the inciting event in your hunt for the buried treasure in your character's past, you'll have a better idea of the type of questions you should be asking.

But you also need to be aware of the *key event*. The key event is the moment your character becomes *engaged* by the inciting event. For example, in most detective stories, the inciting event (the crime) takes place apart from the main character, who doesn't become involved with it until the key event, when he takes on the case. The key event takes place *after* the inciting event, since its job is to build upon the inciting event and make it impossible for the main character to turn away from it.

(For more information on the inciting and key events, see pages 100-103 of *Outlining Your Novel* and pages 81-85 of *Structuring Your Novel.*)

What event starts the plot rolling? (This is your inciting event.) _____

Airplane travel interrupted

How does your inciting event influence the story to follow? _____

it separates Lyle from world to MRO

How does your inciting event create conflict? feeds Lyles

objective

How does your inciting event grab readers' attention? _____

_____.

What event involves your character in the plot? (This is your key event.) _____

_____.

How does your key event influence the story to follow? _____

_____.

How does your key event create conflict? _____

_____.

How does your key event grab readers' attention? _____

_____.

How does your protagonist react to the key event? _____

_____.

What events in the character's past caused the inciting event? _____

_____.

What events in the character's past led him up to the key event? _____

_____.

What shaped the character to make him respond to the inciting and/or key events as he does? _____

_____.

What unresolved issues from his past can further complicate the spiral of events that result from the inciting event? _____

_____.

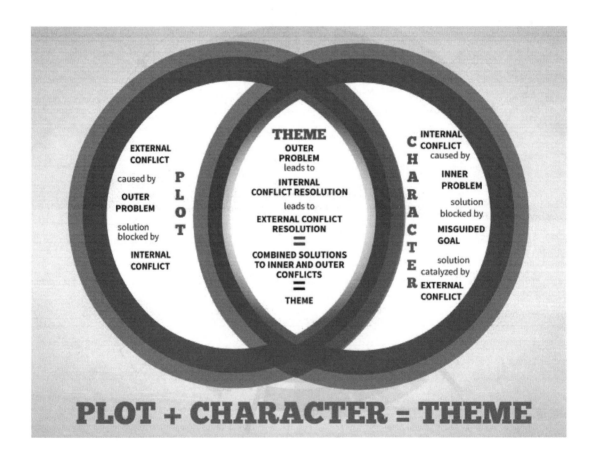

HOW TO WRITE BACKSTORY

ALTHOUGH EVERY DETAIL in your backstory is important, since it contributes to your understanding of your characters and plot, what you're *really* looking for as you explore your character's histories are the epochs, the catalysts, and the notable events that have marked your character's life, for better or worse, in ways he'll never forget.

The deeper you dig, the more likely you are to strike a rich vein, so don't let yourself off easy with a few sentences: "Sam was born in Massachusetts. Married his high-school sweetheart after college. They have two kids. He works as an accountant." That kind of backstory gives you no insight into Sam's character and no treasure trove to fund a luxurious plot.

A relatively small amount of your backstory will show up in the novel, but this kind of in-depth background information provides an incredibly strong foundation. And the bits of backstory that *do* make an appearance will add extra sparkle to your story.

Begin with a general statement about your character.

(For more information about backstory, see pages 103-109 of *Outlining Your Novel*.)

EXAMPLES:

Annan is the hero of our story. He is a hired assassin, a professional soldier, and in general a tough character. Tacit and solid, with the raw strength to more than match three full-grown men, he is a fearsome opponent on any level.

He is currently in the employ of King Richard, as a member of his personal guard. He came to that position by way of Richard's admiration of his fighting prowess at a fight in the lists during the trip East.

Unbeknownst to Richard, Annan has also been offered the job of assassinating either the King himself or the King's new Queen, Berengaria of Navarre. He was approached, before the King's vanguard ever embarked from England, by Bishop Roderic's emissary, and offered a hefty sum for killing the King.
(*Behold the Dawn*)

In a few paragraphs, explain the basic facts about your protagonist and his involvement in your story.

He is the product of a father who is a deity hoping to bring about the end of the world

How old is your protagonist? 17 _____.

When is his birthday? Sept 25 _____.

Where was your protagonist born? _____.

Who is his father? _____.

What's his backstory? _____

_____.

Who is his mother? _____.

What's her backstory? _____

_____.

What values were important to whoever raised him? _____

_____.

Who are your protagonist's siblings? _____

_____.

What are their ages? _____.

Summarize each of their personalities in two words—one positive and one

negative: _____.

Who were the protagonist's early mentors? _____.

What was his economic and social status while growing up? _____.

What's his ethnic background? _____.

In what places has he lived? _____.

What's his level of education? _____.

    What was his favorite subject in school? _____.

    Has he had any special training? _____.

What jobs has he held? _____.

Where has he traveled? _____.

What personal epochs have shaped him? _____

_____.

    What "ghost" hides in his past? What emotional, mental, or physical wound has

    he suffered, prior to the story, that has prompted his belief in the Lie? _____

    _____.

CREATIVE EXERCISE:

Write a scene in which your character's backstory is important, but don't explain the backstory in narrative. Instead, craft your dialogue and subtext so readers can gain all the information they need.

SOMETHING TO THINK ABOUT:

1. Before beginning these exercises, were you already aware of your story's inciting event?
2. Was working backwards from the inciting event to discover your character's backstory helpful? Or would it have been more intuitive to begin with your character's birth and work forward to find the inciting event?
3. How will you work your backstory into your story proper? Will it provide any mystery or suspense?
4. Have you ever had a backstory grow so large it became more interesting than your original story concept?
5. Were you already aware of the differences between the inciting and key events?
6. Do you ever find it difficult to balance the need to explain backstory with the necessity to keep the story proper moving forward?
7. Can you think of stories that did a particularly good job incorporating backstory?

RESOURCES:

- "Improve Your Character Instantly—Just Add a Ghost," K.M. Weiland, helpingwritersbecomeauthors.com/2013/10/improve-your-character-instantly-just
- "Is Your Novel's Backstory Big Enough?" K.M. Weiland, helpingwriters becomeauthors.com/2013/07/is-your-novels-backstory-big-enough
- "When Your Backstory Becomes Your Story," K.M. Weiland, helping writersbecomeauthors.com/2012/02/posts-6
- "How to wield back story with panache," Roz Morris, helpingwriters becomeauthors.com/OYNW-Morris
- "How to Use Subtext in Your Writing," Marianne Vest, helpingwriters becomeauthors.com/OYNW-Vest

4

Character Sketches: Character Interviews

ONE OF THE most useful tools to get your creativity flowing and your characters talking is the "character interview." You can refer to these questions and answers continually throughout the writing process, not only for on-the-spot inspiration, but for fact checking (How old was he when his mother died? Did he break his left or his right leg in that car accident?).

Character interviews are a lengthy process, so you may only want to focus on the point-of-view characters, the antagonist, and maybe one or two important minor characters. This part of the outlining process should get your brain juices foaming and raise all kinds of interesting tangents and opportunities for deepening the plot.

CHARACTER INTERVIEW

A LTHOUGH YOU CAN answer the questions by simply filling in the blanks (e.g., Overall outlook on life? Cynical), you'll allow your imagination more freedom by working the problems out longhand in your notebook so you can write down and flesh out your every idea.

(For more information on character interviews, see pages 115-119 in *Outlining Your Novel.*)

EXAMPLE:

Strongest/weakest character traits: Annan's strong trait is the light of a moral core that refuses to be dampened despite the ashes of sin and despair heaped upon it. There is a line Annan will not cross. He has walked upon it many times, but he will not be pushed over.

He has many weaknesses. His temper, backed by all of his formidable strength and power, is a weapon to be feared. He kills without thought, though, ironically, he is also quick to defend others. He is a man of conundrums. He kills and yet, for some things, he's willing to be killed. He hates, and yet he hates his hatred. He is a man of passion, yet also of discipline.
(*Behold the Dawn*)

Name: _____.

BACKGROUND

Current address and phone number: _____.

Jobs: _____.

    Salary: _____.

Travel: _____.

Friends: _____.

    How do people view this character: _____.

Lives with: _____.

Fights with: _____.

Spends time with: _____.

Wishes to spend time with: _____.

Depends on him: _____.

People he most admires: _____.

Enemies: _____.

Dating, marriage: _____.

Children: _____.

Religious views: _____.

Outlook

Overall outlook on life: _____.

Does this character like himself? _____.

What, if anything, would he change about his life? _____.

Personal demons: _____.

Is he lying to himself about something? _____.

Optimistic/Pessimistic: _____.

Real/Feigned: _____.

Morality level: _____.

Confidence level: _____.

Typical day: _____.

What five words would he use to describe himself?

     1. _____.

     2. _____.

     3. _____.

     4. _____.

     5. _____.

What five words would his best friend use?

     1. _____.

     2. _____.

     3. _____.

     4. _____.

     5. _____.

List the identities of this character (mother, lover, soldier, etc.) in order of

priority to this person:_____.

Degree of self-awareness:
1. ☐ (Not aware at all.)
2. ☐
3. ☐
4. ☐
5. ☐
6. ☐
7. ☐
8. ☐
9. ☐
10. ☐ (Very aware.)

Greatest joy? _____.

Greatest pain? _____.

Things Everyone Knows About the Character	Things Everyone *But* the Character Knows About Him
Things Only the Protagonist Knows About Himself	Things No One Knows Yet That Will Develop During the Story

PHYSICAL APPEARANCE

Physical build: _____.

Posture: _____.

Head shape: _____.

Eyes: _____.

Nose: _____.

Mouth: _____.

Hair: _____.

Skin: _____.

Tattoos/piercings/scars: _____.

Voice: _____.

What people notice first: _____.

Clothing: _____.

How would he describe himself? _____.

Health/disabilities/handicaps: _____.

CHARACTERISTICS

Love language:
- ☐ Gifts
- ☐ Quality Time
- ☐ Words of Affirmation
- ☐ Acts of Service
- ☐ Physical Touch

Strongest/weakest character traits: _____.

How can the flip side of his strong point be a weakness? _____

_____.

How much self-control and self-discipline does he have? _____.

What makes him irrationally angry? _____.

What makes him cry? _____.

Fears: _____.

Talents: _____.

What people like best about him: _____.

INTERESTS AND FAVORITES

Political leaning: _____.

Collections: _____.

Food, drink: _____.

Music: _____.

Books: _____.

Movies: _____.

Sports, recreation: _____.

Did he play in school? _____.

Color: _____.

Best way to spend a weekend: _____.

A great gift for this person: _____.

Pets: _____.

Vehicles: _____.

What large possessions does he own (car, home, furnishings, boat, etc.) and which

does he like best? _____.

TYPICAL EXPRESSIONS AND ATTITUDES

Typical expressions:

When happy: _____.

When angry: _____.

When frustrated: _____.

When sad: _____.

When afraid: _____.

Idiosyncrasies: _____.

Laughs or jeers at: _____.

Ways to cheer up this person: _____.

Ways to annoy this person: _____.

Hopes and dreams: _____.

How does he see himself accomplishing these dreams? _____

_____.

Worst thing he's ever done to someone and why: _____

_____.

Greatest success: _____.

Biggest trauma: _____.

Biggest embarrassment: _____.

Cares about most in the world: _____.

Secrets: _____.

If he could do one thing and succeed at it, what would it be? _____.

He is the kind of person who: _____.

What do you love most about this character? _____.

Why will readers sympathize with this person right away? _____.

How will his voice sound on the page? _____.

How is the character ordinary or extraordinary? _____.

How is his situation ordinary or extraordinary? _____.

Core need: _____.

Anecdote (defining moment): _____

_____.

History: _____

_____

_____

_____

_____

_____

_____

_____

_____

_____

_____

_____

_____.

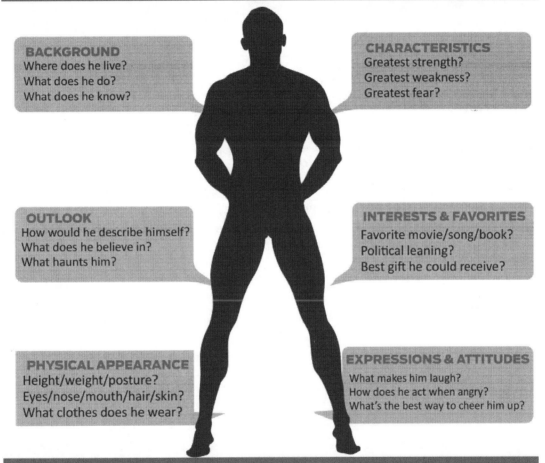

How Well Do You Know Your Character?

BACKGROUND
Where does he live?
What does he do?
What does he know?

CHARACTERISTICS
Greatest strength?
Greatest weakness?
Greatest fear?

OUTLOOK
How would he describe himself?
What does he believe in?
What haunts him?

INTERESTS & FAVORITES
Favorite movie/song/book?
Political leaning?
Best gift he could receive?

PHYSICAL APPEARANCE
Height/weight/posture?
Eyes/nose/mouth/hair/skin?
What clothes does he wear?

EXPRESSIONS & ATTITUDES
What makes him laugh?
How does he act when angry?
What's the best way to cheer him up?

helpingwritersbecomeauthors.com

FREEHAND INTERVIEW

I F YOUR CHARACTER turns out to be the closemouthed type who refuses to let you into his deeper psyche, try a "freehand interview." Instead of forcing your character into the rigidity of the set questions in a regular interview, throw him onto the page and start asking him questions: *What's the matter with you? What are you hiding from me?* It's always surprising how many unexpected confessions you can drag out of your characters.

(For more on freehand interviews, see pages 120-121 of *Outlining Your Novel*.)

EXAMPLE:

Author: Why are you being so uncooperative?

Character: Why are you asking stupid questions?

Author: Because I need you to do what I tell you. I need you to show some fight to your wicked stepmother, instead of just pouting and taking it.

Character: That is *so* easy for you to say. You don't know my stepmother. And besides, I'm not just taking it. Somebody has to do the chores around here and take care of my baby stepsisters. If I don't do it, we'll all die in filthy misery.

Author: _____

_____.

Character: _____

_____

_____.

Author: _____

_____.

Character: _____

_____

_____.

Author: _____

_____ .

Character: _____

_____

_____ .

Author: _____

_____ .

Character: _____

_____

Author: _____

_____ .

Character: _____

_____

_____ .

Author: _____

_____ .

Character: _____

_____

_____ .

Author: _____

_____.

Character: _____

_____

_____.

Author: _____

_____.

Character: _____

_____

_____.

Author: _____

_____.

Character: _____

_____

_____.

Author: _____

_____.

Character: _____

_____

_____.

PERSONALITY PROFILING

PERSONALITY PROFILING IS another tool you can use to discover your character. You'll find many variations and approaches to personality types, including the predominant Myers-Briggs Type Indicator, the Four Temperaments approach, and the Enneagram. Making use of these guides can be invaluable in creating realistic characters.

(Note: In *Outlining Your Novel*, I stated I disliked personality typing systems because they might stunt organic character evolution. However, I now believe personality typing can be a tremendous tool for creating realistic characters.)

(For more on personality profiling, see pages 121-122 of *Outlining Your Novel*.)

MYERS-BRIGGS TYPE INDICATOR

The Myers-Briggs system of personality profiling breaks down personalities into sixteen divisions, based on four categories of two choices each, pertaining to how people process information and interact with the world. Out of each of the following pairs, choose which option best suits your character. Write the corresponding letter in the blanks at the bottom of the page to discover the "code" for his personality. To learn what his code reveals, as well as more about each personality type and how the Myers-Briggs system works, visit helpingwritersbecomeauthors.com/OYNW-Myers-Briggs. To read Myers-Briggs profiles of popular characters, visit helpingwriters becomeauthors.com/OYNW-Bishop.

EXAMPLES:

- Tony Stark in *Iron Man* is an ENTJ (the Leader).

- Pip in Charles Dickens's *Great Expectations* is an ISFP (the Artist).

- James Kirk in *Star Trek* is an ESTP (the Adventurer).

Favorite world: Does your character prefer to focus on the outer world (Extroversion: **E**) or on his own inner world (Introversion: **I**)?

Information: Does your character prefer to focus on the basic information he takes in (Sensing: **S**), or does he prefer to interpret and add meaning (Intuition: **N**)?

Decisions: When making decisions, does your character prefer to first look at consistent logic (Thinking: **T**), or does he look at people and circumstances (Feeling: **F**)?

Structure: In dealing with the outside world, does your character prefer to make decisions quickly (Judging: J), or does he prefer to stay open to new information and options (Perceiving: P)?   _____ _____ _____ _____

FOUR TEMPERAMENTS

THE ANCIENT "FOUR temperaments" approach (popularized by Tim LaHaye, among others) narrows personalities into four basic categories: choleric, melancholic, sanguine, and phlegmatic. Read the following descriptions and put a check next to whichever best suits your character.

(For more information on the Four Temperaments, see *Why You Act the Way You Do* by Tim LaHaye.)

EXAMPLES:

- **Emma Woodhouse is choleric.**
  (*Emma* by Jane Austen)

- **Ender Wiggin is melancholic.**
  (*Ender's Game* by Orson Scott Card)

- **Mike Wazowski is sanguine.**
  (*Monsters, Inc.* directed by Pete Docter)

- **Steve Rogers is phlegmatic.**
  (*Captain America: The First Avenger* directed by Joe Johnston)

☐ Choleric

Cholerics don't do much of anything halfway. They thunder through life at top speed, which is both their greatest strength and their greatest weakness. They're determined, aggressive, and productive. They're "good enough" people. Perfectionism doesn't cripple them, but that can mean they don't always complete jobs as well as they should. They can also be disorganized, impatient, and overbearing. They're usually extroverts and often leaders.

☐ Melancholic

Melancholics are arguably the most talented of all the personalities. They often have a natural bent toward artistic expression. They're detail-oriented, patient, and idealistic. But in spite of all their talent, they're often prone to feelings of insecurity and self-doubt. Their perfectionism and mood swings can cause them to feel they never measure up, which can, in turn, keep them from completing projects. They're usually introverts.

☐ **Sanguine**

Sanguines are the bubbly extroverts who bring life to any party. They're fun and funny, sociable and charismatic. These folks know how to tell a good story—with all the dramatic flourishes. They're often compassionate and emotional (in both the good and bad senses of the word). However, they can also be unorganized and undependable, which can lead to difficulties in creating consistent schedules and finishing projects.

☐ **Phlegmatic**

Phlegmatics are the Steady Eddies. They're not easily ruffled, which means they get to avoid many of the high and low mood swings to which the other personality types can be prone. They're dependable, thoughtful, pragmatic, and usually introverted. But they can also struggle to find motivation and energy to start—and then finish—projects.

ENNEAGRAM

THE ENNEAGRAM IS a typology of human personalities that aligns character traits with nine categories. The enneagram can help you round out a character, summarize his personality, and identify his "fatal flaw."

(For more information on the Enneagram, visit helpingwritersbecome authors.com/OYNW-Campbell.)

EXAMPLES:

- Scarlett O'Hara is a Four.
- Sherlock Holmes is a Five.
- Han Solo is a Seven.

Ennegram Chart

Type	Ideal	Fear	Desire	Vice
1: Reformer	Perfection	Corruption	Integrity	Anger
2: Helper	Freedom	Unworthiness	Love	Vainglory
3: Achiever	Hope	Worthlessness	Being valued	Deceit
4: Individual	Origin	Commonness	Authenticity	Envy
5: Investigator	Omniscience	Uselessness	Competency	Avarice
6: Loyalist	Faith	Isolation	Safety	Fear
7: Enthusiast	Work	Boredom	Experiences	Gluttony
8: Challenger	Truth	Loss of control	Autonomy	Lust
9: Peacemaker	Love	Loss	Stability	Indifference

LIKABLE CHARACTER CHECKLIST

MAKE READERS LIKE your character, and they will follow him to the center of the earth. If they like your character, they won't just read your book, they'll ache when it's over, buy it in hard cover just so they never have to say goodbye, re-read it until it's dog-eared, and welcome that character to a permanent place in their hearts.

Likable characters require careful crafting if they're to come to life in a way that is not only believable but compelling. Likable does not equal perfect. Goody two-shoes will more probably inspire a gag reflex than undying loyalty. Likable characters come in all shapes and sizes. Some are blatantly endearing. Some make us like them in spite of their flaws.

Answer the following questions to help polish your protagonist's likability.

1. What **actions** will characterize your protagonist? _____

_____.

2. How can your protagonist represent the **moral** vision of right and wrong, as

shared by most people? _____

_____.

3. How can your protagonist demonstrate **selflessness**? _____

_____.

4. How can your protagonist demonstrate **competence**? _____

_____.

5. Which other characters will **love** your protagonist? _____

_____.

6. How can your protagonist demonstrate **bravery**? _____

_____.

7. How can your protagonist demonstrate **determination**? _____

_____.

8. Which of your protagonist's goals, dreams, or desires will readers be able to **relate** to?

_____.

9. How can your protagonist demonstrate **wit**? _____

_____.

10. How can your protagonist show **kindness** to others? _____

_____.

List your character's three most prominent traits (e.g., Hoss Cartwright's strength) and at least one way you can use each trait in the story.

Trait #1: _____.

How will you demonstrate it? _____.

Trait #2: _____.

How will you demonstrate it? _____.

Trait #3: _____.

How will you demonstrate it? _____.

Minor Characters

FOR EACH OF your prominent minor characters, answer the following questions:

Name: _____.

Occupation: _____.

Unique or unexpected trait: _____.

Life goal: _____.

Plot goal: _____.

Stakes: _____.

Changes in personality or status by end of book: _____.

Name: _____.

Occupation: _____.

Unique or unexpected trait: _____.

Life goal: _____.

Plot goal: _____.

Stakes: _____.

Changes in personality or status by end of book: _____.

Name: _____.

Occupation: _____.

Unique or unexpected trait: _____.

Life goal: _____.

Plot goal: _____.

Stakes: _____.

Changes in personality or status by end of book: _____.

Name: _____.

Occupation: _____.

Unique or unexpected trait: _____.

Life goal: _____.

Plot goal: _____.

Stakes: _____.

Changes in personality or status by end of book: _____.

CREATIVE EXERCISE:

Write a scene in which your main character does not appear, but in which two or more characters discuss him. Do you learn anything surprising about your character?

SOMETHING TO THINK ABOUT:

1. Do you feel your character embodies most of the ten "likable" traits on pages 85-86?
2. Do you think there's any fear of your protagonist endangering the conflict by becoming too nice?
3. How will you develop your minor characters to ensure they're three-dimensional?
4. What qualities make your favorite characters memorable?
5. Have you ever written a character based on yourself or someone you know?
6. Did your current story originate with a character idea or a plot idea?

RESOURCES:

- "Why Nice Characters Equal No Conflict," K.M. Weiland, helpingwriters becomeauthors.com/2011/06/why-nice-characters-equal-no-conflict
- "5 Steps to Dazzling Minor Characters," K.M. Weiland, helpingwriters becomeauthors.com/2010/08/5-steps-to-dazzling-minor-characters
- "What makes a sympathetic hero?," Jason Black, helpingwritersbecome authors.com/OYNW-Black
- "9 character qualities that generate support," Darcy Pattison, helping writersbecomeauthors.com/OYNW-Pattison
- "The Character Traits Thesaurus," Writers Helping Writers, helpingwriters becomeauthors.com/OYNW-Thesaurus

5
SETTING

SETTING IS SOMETIMES the neglected stepchild of the writing world. We lavish attention on our characters and plot, but we don't always remember how powerful a fabulous setting can be.

Depending on the type of story you're writing, the setting may start out as little more than an afterthought, an arbitrary decision made simply because your characters have to live *somewhere*. In the best stories, however, setting is an inherent element in bringing to life not just the scenery but the characters themselves. As such, it isn't something you can afford to overlook.

SETTING QUESTIONS

Ask yourself the following questions to strengthen the weak points in your setting construction and to help you use it to its full potential.

(For more information about settings, see pages 127-130 in *Outlining Your Novel*.)

What is your story's primary setting? _____.

Is your setting inherent to your plot? _____.

If you changed the setting, how would it change the plot? _____

_____.

How does your character view his setting? _____

_____.

How does your setting affect the story's tone? _____

_____.

List ten interesting sub-settings within your main setting.

EXAMPLES:

- In Stephen King's *Rita Hayworth and the Shawshank Redemption*, the main setting is a prison, but sub-settings include the library, the various cells, and the warden's office.

- In Christopher Nolan's *Batman Begins*, the main setting is Gotham City, but sub-settings include Wayne Manor, Wayne Tower, and Arkham Asylum.

- In George Lucas's *Star Wars*, the main setting is a galaxy far, far away, but sub-settings include Tatooine, which includes the sub-settings of the Lars homestead, Mos Eisley spaceport, and Jabba's palace.

1. _____.

2. _____.

3. _____.

4. _____.

5. _____.

6. _____.

7. _____.

8. _____.

9. _____.

10. _____.

Which of these would work for your story? _____.

What setting will you use for your climactic showdown? _____.

How will this setting reflect the protagonist's inner battle? _____

_____.

How will this setting amplify the conflict (e.g., if the conflict is physical, the setting

might present physical obstacles)? _____

_____.

How can you make the spaces in the climactic setting smaller to force your protagonist
and antagonist together? _____

_____.

How can this setting add to your protagonist's discomfort—physically or emotionally?

_____.

How can you foreshadow your climactic setting earlier in the book? _____

_____.

SETTING CHECKLIST

☐ Is the setting memorable?

☐ Does it strengthen theme, either through unity or by contrast?

☐ Do the settings for each of the primary plot points (see page 110) allow you to make these scenes as exciting and resonant as possible?

☐ Does your setting contain your story by keeping it within the bounds of an established place (e.g., N.Y.C., China, or outer space)?

☐ Do the settings in the beginning and ending frame your story by either mirroring or contrasting each other?

☐ Is your setting familiar and/or interesting to you?

HOW
DO YOU KNOW YOU'VE CHOSEN THE RIGHT CLIMACTIC SETTING?

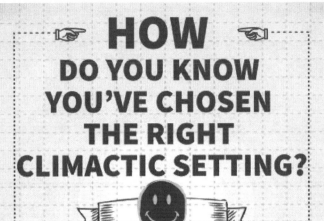

Logical for the Plot + Previously Featured and/or Foreshadowed + Thematically Resonant + Emotionally Traumatizing for Protagonist + Physically Confining =

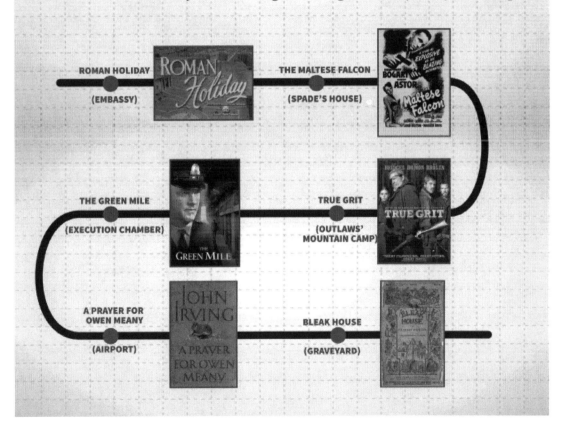

ROMAN HOLIDAY
(EMBASSY)

THE MALTESE FALCON
(SPADE'S HOUSE)

THE GREEN MILE
(EXECUTION CHAMBER)

TRUE GRIT
(OUTLAWS' MOUNTAIN CAMP)

A PRAYER FOR OWEN MEANY
(AIRPORT)

BLEAK HOUSE
(GRAVEYARD)

SETTINGS LIST

LIST ALL THE settings you know about in this story. As you continue to outline your story, flip back to this section and write down every new setting you add. When you're finished, examine your list. Could you eliminate or combine any of the settings? Could you choose more exciting, colorful, or resonant settings for any of your scenes?

1. _____.

2. _____.

3. _____.

4. _____.

5. _____.

6. _____.

7. _____.

8. _____.

9. _____.

10. _____.

11. _____.

12. _____.

13. _____.

14. _____.

15. _____.

WORLD BUILDING

IN MANY GENRES, the setting is little more than a necessary backdrop, culled from the author's real life or research for any number of reasons. But if you're embarking into the magical world of fantasy, you will be presented with a wonderful new opportunity: you will no longer be constrained by the facts. Instead, you have the freedom to create an entirely new world where anything could happen.

In the face of all these possibilities, authors can easily become overwhelmed. Where do we start? How do we create a world that not only incorporates beautiful and fascinatingly bizarre elements, but also one that is solid and realistic in every detail, from landscape to government? The first, and hopefully most obvious, answer is to let your imagination run riot. Force yourself to think outside the box, to reject clichés, and to hunt down ideas that excite you with their color and originality.

But you're also going to want to be as specific as you can. The interview process you used in getting to know your characters can also be applied to your setting. Answer the following questions about your speculative setting.

(For more information about world building, refer to Patricia C. Wrede's "Fantasy Worldbuilding Questions" by visiting helpingwritersbecomeauthors.com/OYNW-Wrede.)

What does the landscape look like? _____

_____.

What kinds of plants grow here? _____

_____.

What's the climate? _____

_____.

What animals are present in this world? _____

_____.

What societies are found in this world? _____

_____.

What kinds of clothing are in style? _____

_____.

What moral and religious values define people's world views? _____

_____.

What language(s) do they speak? _____

_____.

What form of government is currently in place? _____

_____.

How advanced is technology? _____

_____.

What forms of long-distance communication are used? _____

_____.

What modes of transportation are available? _____

_____.

How has technology affected entertainment and the arts? _____

_____.

How has technology affected weaponry and warfare? _____

_____.

How advanced are the fields of medicine and science? _____

_____.

What are the natural laws of this world? _____

_____.

Which natural laws are different from our world (e.g., gravity)? _____

_____.

Is there a magical force in your world? How does it work? What are its limitations?

_____.

What kinds of people populate this world? _____

_____.

Are there different races? _____

_____.

How do customs differ between people of different races and citizens of different

districts? _____

_____.

Do the ethnic factions get along? _____

_____.

What's the history of this world? _____

_____.

How many years of recorded history are available? _____

_____.

What historical epochs have shaped society? _____

_____.

CREATIVE EXERCISE:

Imagine your story taking place in a very different setting from your original conception (e.g., L.A. instead of Kansas, China instead of America, Mars instead of Earth, the Dark Ages instead of modern times). Write a list of ways this would both improve and damage your premise.

SOMETHING TO THINK ABOUT:

1. Did you know what your primary setting would be right from the beginning of your story's conception? Why or why not?

2. How does your setting strengthen or contrast your protagonist's conflict with the antagonist?

3. How does your setting strengthen or contrast your protagonist's inner struggle?

4. Is your story's primary setting one taken from real life, one you made up, or a little of both?

5. When you think back on the vivid moments in some of your favorite stories, are the settings clear in your mind?

6. Even if you don't write speculative fiction, do you think the list of world-building questions on pages 97-100 could be helpful in fleshing out your real-world setting?

RESOURCES:

- "One Thing the Movies Can Teach You About Setting," K.M. Weiland, helpingwritersbecomeauthors.com/2008/01/one-thing-movies-can-teach-you-about

- "Illustrate Your Character Through His Surroundings," K.M. Weiland, helpingwritersbecomeauthors.com/2011/07/illustrate-your-character-through-his

- "The Case of the Vanishing Setting," K.M. Weiland, helpingwritersbecome authors.com/2012/02/most-common-mistakes-series-case-of

- "Creating Unforgettable Settings," Writers Helping Writers, helpingwriters becomeauthors.com/OYNW-Ackerman

- "Why You Need to Focus on Description," Joe Bunting, helpingwriters becomeauthors.com/OYNW-Bunting2

6
EXTENDED OUTLINE

THE EXTENDED OUTLINE is where your plotting begins in earnest. Step by step, you're going to map out, in as much detail as possible (though without dialogue or narrative), every road stop in your story. In places, this plotting will go quickly; in others, you'll have to stop to work your way through iffy plot points and implausible character motivations. This step will probably take longer to complete than any of the previous steps, but because of the active, full-throttle creativity it demands, it's one of the most exciting and rewarding portions of storytelling.

STORY ELEMENTS

NOW IS THE time to begin making concrete decisions about the form your story will take. What audience are you writing it for? What feel and tone do you want to present in the prose? Will it be fast-paced or leisurely? Will you write in past or present tense?

What is *your* perfect novel? Examine your favorite novels and movies for elements that particularly grabbed you. Battle scenes? Romance? Humorous dialogue? Plot twists? Sad endings? Happy endings? Chances are the story elements that are important to you are already showing up in your work. If you can single them out, you can strengthen them and make them more intrinsic to your stories. List four of your favorite books and movies. Beneath each title, identify your three favorite elements within each story.

(For more information on identifying the kind of story you're writing, see pages 142-145 of *Outlining Your Novel*.)

EXAMPLE:

Master and Commander by Patrick O'Brian
Favorite Elements: Friendship between main characters, subtle humor, historical detail

1. _____.

    Favorite Elements: _____.

2. _____.

    Favorite Elements: _____.

3. _____.

    Favorite Elements: _____.

4. _____.

    Favorite Elements: _____.

Which elements show up in all or most of the titles? _____

_____.

How can you incorporate these elements into your book? _____

_____.

If your book were a movie, what category would it fall into (e.g., chick flick, summer

blockbuster, Oscar bait)? _____.

How can you incorporate humor into this story? _____

_____.

What kind of action will be present in your story? _____

_____.

What relationships will your story focus on? _____

_____.

Voice and POV

NARRATIVE POINT OF view (or POV) is something writers often take for granted. We come up with a story idea, sit down to write, and spend maybe all of thirty seconds debating between a first- and third-person POV. But this decision will influence every one of the 100,000-plus words to follow. It will be a deciding factor in the story's tone and narrative arc. It will control which scenes will be written and which will remain "off-camera." It will close certain doors and open others. In short, POV is often the single most important factor in determining whether or not a story *works*.

The character you choose as your main POV will influence the tone of the entire novel. It's often wise to look beyond the obvious choice of POV and see what your other characters have to offer. Don't be afraid to play around with voice and tone. Start by answering the following questions.

(For more information on voice and POV, see pages 143-145 in *Outlining Your Novel*.)

Which characters will be narrators? _____

_third-person deep point of view_____.

Could you eliminate the POV of any of these characters without dramatically

affecting the story? _____.

Which character has the most at stake? _____.

Is this character your primary narrator? Why or why not? _____

_____.

In what person will you tell the story?

- ☒ Third-person (*Mac went to the store.*)
- ☐ First-person (*I went to the store.*) — deep
- ☐ Second-person (*You went to the store.*)
- ☒ Omniscient (*Mac went to the store, little knowing Arthur was already there.*)

In what tense will you tell the story?

☑ Past (*Mac opened the door.*)
☐ Present (*Mac opens the door.*)

Write a paragraph from the perspective of each of your potential narrators:

Character Name: _____

Voice Test: _____

_____

_____

_____.

Character Name: _____

Voice Test: _____

_____

_____

_____.

Character Name: _____

Voice Test: _____

_____

_____

_____.

Character Name: _____

Voice Test: _____

_____

_____

_____.

Character Name: _____

Voice Test: _____

_____

_____

_____.

Which of these characters have the most interesting voices? _____

_____.

IDENTIFYING YOUR AUDIENCE

IT'S ESSENTIAL TO know your audience and what they expect from you. When, how, and if you decide to fulfill those expectations need to be educated decisions. Sometimes it helps to select one person—someone who understands you and your worldview, but who perhaps doesn't agree with you entirely. What would this friend think of your story? What would he like about it? Dislike? What would he tell you to change to make the story better? Hold this one reader in mind as you design your outline, and you'll be able to stay in touch with your intended audience, as a whole, as you craft your story.

Answer the following questions to identify your audience.

How old is your audience? _Young Adult_.

What gender is your audience? _All genders_.

What ethnicity is your audience? _All ethnicities_.

What religious beliefs does your audience ascribe to? _All or most religions_

STORY STRUCTURE

STRUCTURE IS THE most important technical aspect of any story. It brings solidity and focus. It's a roadmap—a time-tested archetype for crafting the rise and fall of action and character evolution within your story.

At its most basic level, structure is about timing. Structure ensures things happen in a story—things your main character can react to—and it ensures these things happen at just the right moment to rivet your readers' attention and give them the biggest bang for their buck. You're free to rev your imagination into high gear and be as wild and creative as you want. But you also get to rely on a structural "cheat sheet" of sorts, which will guide you in molding your plot into a lean, mean, storytelling machine.

The classic approach to structure divides story into three acts. As you begin outlining your story, answer the following questions to make sure you're making the most of your story's structure. If you don't know all the answers yet, return to fill in the blanks when you do.

(For more information on story structure, see *Structuring Your Novel: Essential Keys for Writing an Outstanding Story*.)

FIRST ACT

What is your hook? _____.

What implicit or explicit question will immediately pique readers' curiosity? _____

_____.

What "characteristic moment" introduces your protagonist? _____

_____.

What is the protagonist's "normal world"? _____

_____.

What is your character doing in the first scene that allows him to be physically moving?

_____.

Why will readers care about or empathize with your protagonist? _____

_____.

What does your protagonist want in the beginning? _____

_____.

What does he believe he must accomplish in order to achieve his goal? _____

_____.

Who or what opposes this goal? _____

_____.

What is at stake if he doesn't reach his goal? _____

_____.

How will you introduce the other important characters? _____

_____.

What is the inciting event? _____

_____.

What is the key event? _____

_____.

How will the first major plot point at the end of the First Act force your character to leave his "normal world" and engage in the conflict with the antagonistic force?

_____

_____.

Second Act

How does the protagonist react to the first plot point at the end of the First Act? __

_____.

How are the spiral of events at this point outside the protagonist's control? _____

_____.

How will you force the protagonist's original goal out of his reach? _____

_____.

What new goals arise in response to the conflict? _____

_____.

What "pinch point" will occur approximately ¼ into the Second Act to showcase

the antagonistic force's power? _____

_____.

What "centerpiece" event at the midpoint will force your protagonist to stop reacting

to the antagonistic force and start acting? _____

_____.

How will the midpoint grant the protagonist a clearer understanding of the conflict

and his own reactions to it? _____

_____.

After the midpoint, how will the protagonist shift into a more active and in-control response to the antagonistic force? _____

_____.

What "pinch point" will occur approximately ¾ into the Second Act to showcase the antagonistic force's power and foreshadow the climax? _____

_____.

How will the protagonist seem to achieve victory at the end of the Second Act? ___

_____.

THIRD ACT

What new defeat at the third plot point will force the protagonist to a personal low?

_____.

How will the protagonist respond to this defeat? _____

_____.

What will be the protagonist's renewed response to the antagonist? _____

_____.

How will the protagonist confront the antagonist during the climax? _____

_____.

Where will the climax take place? _____

_____.

What happens to the protagonist during the climax? _____

_____.

What happens to the antagonist during the climax? _____

_____.

What is the climactic moment? _____

_____.

What loose ends need to be tied up in the resolution? _____

_____.

How can your ending scene reflect elements of your opening scene?

Opening scene: _____

_____.

Closing scene: _____

_____.

Periods

Reaction	The protagonist reacts to the Key Event and 1st Plot Point.
Action	The protagonist takes action (aggression, decision, inner revelation, etc). Some problems will be solved, but major ones will remain.
Increased Pace	The pacing will naturally increase (and chapter length will decrease) as we approach the Climax.
Climax	The final 10% of the novel, where the core conflict between the protagonist and antagonist is brought to a conclusion.
Resolution	A brief hint (a scene or two) of how the story continues beyond the novel's scope. A period of emotional recovery. A chance to spend another brief moment with the protagonist.

Points

1st Plot Point	A change of surroundings. A personal turning point. The point of no return for the protagonist.
1st Pinch Point	The antagonist's presence and power are displayed.
Turning Point	The midpoint. The turning point of the novel. A change of direction for the characters. A push from reaction to action. A personal catalyst for the protagonist. A move to dramatic, new, fresh, different circumstances.
2nd Pinch Point	The antagonist's presence and power are reaffirmed.
3rd Plot Point	We are set upon our inexorable course towards the Climax. A low point for the protagonist. Perhaps a meeting between protagonist and antagonist? A decision? An upheaval? An unexpected event?

Events

Hook	Grab the reader, provoke interest, and cause questions to be asked.
Inciting Event	The event that sets the story in motion, and will lead to the Key Event.
Key Event	The event that causes the protagonist to be caught up in the story.
Strong Reaction	The protagonist has a strong response to the 1st Plot Point.
Strong Action	The protagonist takes a strong action after the Turning Point.
Climactic Moment	The critical moment that fulfils the dramatic promise of the story.

Chart created by Matt Gemmel • mattgemmel.com • @MattGemmel

SCENE CHECKLIST

THE TIME HAS come to write your Extended Outline. Because of the potential length of this outline, you won't be transcribing your outline directly into the workbook. Grab a notebook or open a computer document. Date each entry and number each scene.

Feel free to ramble, digress, switch tenses, reject ideas, and generally let yourself wander all over your imagination, having fun and seeking plot solutions that are both plausible and unexpected. Using what you've already learned about your story in this workbook, you'll want to plan foreshadowing and sort out the whereabouts and mindsets of your various characters, keeping their motives and goals at the forefront.

Your objective in constructing each scene is to nail down the prominent events. If an appropriate line of dialogue or snippet of description strikes you, go ahead and include it, but, otherwise, save the detail work (such as dialogue, description, and internal narrative) for the first draft.

As you complete each scene, refer to the following list of questions to make sure you're maximizing the scene's potential for the story.

(For more information on the Extended Outline, see pages 139-169 in *Outlining Your Novel*.)

How does this scene lead into the next scene? _____

_____.

How vital is this scene to the story?

    ☐ If I deleted it, the story wouldn't work.
    ☐ It includes only a few important details.
    ☐ The story makes sense without it.

On a scale of 1-10, how excited are you about writing this scene?

☐ 1. ☐ 2. ☐ 3. ☐ 4. ☐ 5. ☐ 6. ☐ 7. ☐ 8. ☐ 9. ☐ 10.

Why does this scene matter to you? _____

_____.

Why will this scene matter to readers? _____

_____.

What new information does this scene introduce? _____

_____.

What old information does this scene reiterate? _____

_____.

On a scale of 1-10, how high are the stakes in this scene?

☐ 1. ☐ 2. ☐ 3. ☐ 4. ☐ 5. ☐ 6. ☐ 7. ☐ 8. ☐ 9. ☐ 10.

On a scale of 1-10, how high is the conflict in this scene?

☐ 1. ☐ 2. ☐ 3. ☐ 4. ☐ 5. ☐ 6. ☐ 7. ☐ 8. ☐ 9. ☐ 10.

Have you included the character's reaction to each scene's main event?

☐ Yes ☐ No

CREATIVE EXERCISE:

Try outlining one of your scenes backwards. Start with where you know you want the scene to end, then work backwards to figure out what the characters logically have to do to reach that conclusion.

SOMETHING TO THINK ABOUT:

1. Was it easy or difficult to identify the major moments in your story's structure?
2. As you're exploring your scenes in your Extended Outline, do you find that you tend to be brief in your descriptions, or do you spend pages searching through the possibilities?
3. Were you previously familiar with the basics of the three-act story structure?
4. Do you believe story structure is important to a successful book? Or do you think it confines creativity?

RESOURCES:

- *Screenplay*, Syd Field
- *Story Engineering*, Larry Brooks
- *Techniques of the Selling Writer*, Dwight V. Swain
- "The Plot Thickens," C.S. Lakin, helpingwritersbecomeauthors.com/OYNW-Lakin
- "A Law of Physics—Err, Writing," Linda Yezak, helpingwritersbecome authors.com/OYNW-Yezak

7
UNCONVENTIONAL OUTLINES

OUTLINES COME IN many shapes and sizes. Keep in mind that your writing process will continually evolve, sometimes without your even realizing it. Different stories will require slightly (or sometimes radically) different tactics. Don't box yourself into a rigid system. Never be afraid to experiment.

Ultimately, finding the right outlining method isn't so much about *choosing* as it is about *creating*. If you're continually striving to learn about the outlining environment that allows you to work most efficiently, you'll be able to refine your writing in ways that reach far beyond the craft itself.

Some stories may demand deviations from the standard "list" outline, in which authors compile a linear list of scenes. Linearity is a great way to make sense of convoluted problems (and the novel is often a very convoluted problem), but sometimes it's worthwhile to use less common forms of outlining as a way of looking at a problem from a new perspective. In this section, we'll explore several unique outlining tools.

Mind Map

MIND MAPS ARE valuable in looking at problems spatially instead of linearly. Don't censor yourself. Write down any related topic that presents itself. This method is particularly useful in breaking through blocks, since it taps both your subconscious and your visual mind.

Start by writing the central idea or event at the middle of the paper and surrounding it with clusters of related subjects—and those subjects with related subjects of their own—until you have created an exhaustive list of possibilities for your story.

(For more information on mind maps, see page 35 in *Outlining Your Novel*.)

EXAMPLE:

Based on *Dreamlander* outline notes.

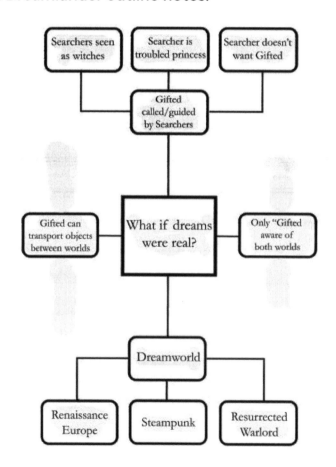

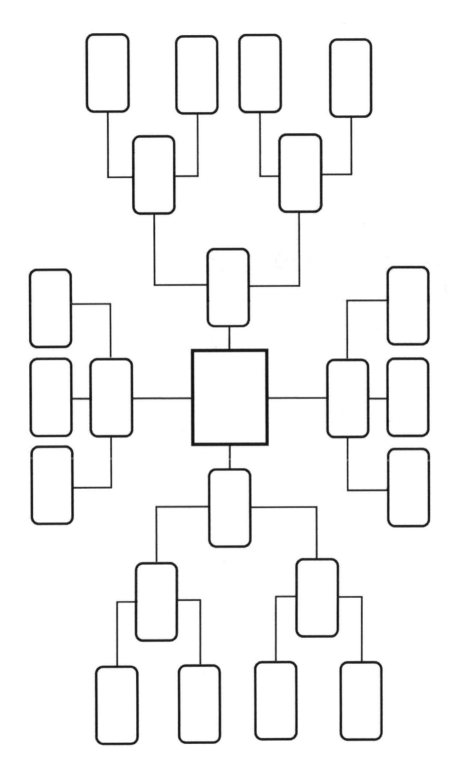

MAP

A LITTLE AMATEUR cartography can be an integral part of world building, even for stories grounded firmly in reality. Because a good setting is inherent to the structure of the story, a map can become a valuable asset in fleshing out your story. Fortunately, artistic talent isn't a requirement for an author's maps. Straight lines to indicate borders, wavy lines for oceans, and spiky triangles for mountains work just fine.

Draw a map of your story's main setting on the opposite page.

(For more information on maps, see page 36 in *Outlining Your Novel*.)

Map of: <u>I celand crash site</u>

Is it a:

☐ World ☐ Continent ☐ Country ☐ City ☒ Building ☐ Other _____

Scale: ☐ quarter inch ☐ half inch ☐ inch ☐ other _____

=

☐ 1 foot ☐ 1 yard ☐ 1 mile ☐ 10 miles ☐ 100 miles ☐ other _____

KEY:

Add your own symbols in the blanks.

- - - - - - - - = Road   X   = City

^^^^^^^^^^ = Mountains   _____ = _____

_____ = _____   _____ = _____

_____ = _____

_____ = _____

_____ = _____

PERFECT REVIEW

YOU'RE NEVER GOING to be completely objective about your stories. But here's a little trick to narrow the gap between the idealization of your story and its printed reality: Write yourself the "perfect" review before your story ever hits paper.

If you could have a professional reviewer read your idealized concept of your finished book and totally *get it*—completely understand everything you're trying to say with your characters, plot, dialogue, and themes—what would he write about your story? Close your eyes for a moment, emotionally distance yourself from your story, and pretend you're that reviewer. Start by answering the following questions as thoroughly and explicitly as possible.

(For more information on writing the perfect review, see pages 36-37 in *Outlining Your Novel.*)

Why did you love reading this story? _____

_____.

What were the best parts? _____

_____.

What is unique about this story? _____

_____.

What was your opinion of the plot? _____

_____.

What was your opinion of the pacing? _____

_____.

What was your opinion of the characters? _____

_____.

Why did you love the protagonist's character arc? _____

_____.

Which character was your favorite? _____

_____.

CALENDAR

WHEN CAUGHT UP in the grand whirl of plotting, you can get carried away and lose track of the time (in more ways than one). Use a twelve-month calendar to choose an appropriate month for your novel's events and start blocking out days. In most fiction, the actual dates won't matter; however, if you're writing historical fiction, which requires adherence to certain dates—and therefore agreement between dates and days of the week—choose a calendar page that accommodates this.

In each appropriate calendar block, scribble a phrase pertaining to the main event of that day (e.g., Party; Funeral; Traveling). The notes need not be extensive, since you can refer to your main outline for more details whenever necessary.

Use the calendar page, opposite, to outline your story's timeline. When you run out of space, find a calendar. Banks and other businesses often provide free calendars upon request, or you can use free online services such as Google Calendar.

(For more information on using calendars in your outline, see page 40 in *Outlining Your Novel*.)

EXAMPLE:

Month: August Year: 1920						
Sun	**Mon**	**Tue**	**Wed**	**Thu**	**Fri**	**Sat**
|1| Woman falls from sky onto biplane	|2| Little boy finds "angel"	|3| Sheriff threatens barnstormer	|4| Airshow qualifying round	|5| Selling plane rides	|6| Airshow	|7| Fight with brother
☐	☐	☐	☐	☐	☐	☐
☐	☐	☐	☐	☐	☐	☐
☐	☐	☐	☐	☐	☐	☐
☐	☐	☐	☐	☐	☐	☐

Month:_____ Year:_____						
Sun	Mon	Tue	Wed	Thu	Fri	Sat
☐	☐	☐	☐	☐	☐	☐
☐	☐	☐	☐	☐	☐	☐
☐	☐	☐	☐	☐	☐	☐
☐	☐	☐	☐	☐	☐	☐
☐	☐	☐	☐	☐	☐	☐

PLAYLISTS

EVERY TIME YOU hear a song that fits your story or inspires some new aspect, save it on a playlist. Find a theme song that embodies each of your characters. Whenever you need a dab of inspiration, give it a listen. Plus, it's great fun for sharing with your readers when the book is published. Create your own personalized story soundtrack!

Novel Theme Song: _____

Protagonist Theme Song: _____

Antagonist Theme Song: _____

Love Interest Theme Song: _____

Sidekick Theme Song: _____

Mentor Theme Song: _____

Opening Chapter Song: _____

First Act/Normal World Song: _____

First Plot Point/Life-Changing Song: _____

First Half of Second Act/Off-Balance Song: _____

Midpoint/Moment of Truth Song: _____

Second Half of Second Act/Taking Action Song: _____

Third Plot Point/Low Moment Song: _____

Third Act/Determination Song: _____

Climax/Final Battle Song: _____

Resolution/Closing Credits Song: _____

OTHER SONGS:

Song Title: _____

    Notes: _____

Song Title: _____

    Notes: _____

Song Title: _____

    Notes: _____

Song Title: _____

    Notes: _____

Song Title: _____

    Notes: _____

Song Title: _____

    Notes: _____

Song Title: _____

    Notes: _____

CAST YOUR CHARACTERS

WE ALL DREAM of getting our *NYT*-bestselling book made into a blockbuster movie. So why wait on the all-important decision of choosing which actors should play your characters? Putting familiar faces, voices, and gestures to your characters can work wonders for bringing them to vivid three-dimensional life. Cast your characters below.

Protagonist: _____

Antagonist: _____

Love Interest: _____

Sidekick: _____

Mentor: _____

OTHER CHARACTERS

Character Name: _____

    Casting Choice: _____

Character Name: _____

    Casting Choice: _____

Character Name: _____

    Casting Choice: _____

Character Name: _____

    Casting Choice: _____

Character Name: _____

    Casting Choice: _____

Character Name: _____

    Casting Choice: _____

Character Name: _____

    Casting Choice: _____

Character Name: _____

    Casting Choice: _____

Character Name: _____

    Casting Choice: _____

Character Name: _____

    Casting Choice: _____

Character Name: _____

    Casting Choice: _____

Character Name: _____

    Casting Choice: _____

Character Name: _____

    Casting Choice: _____

CONCLUSION

SEVERAL YEARS AGO, I had the chance to visit the Victorian Alps in Australia. It was an amazing opportunity, and in hindsight, it was easily one of the best and most educative experiences of my life (not in small part because it was on that trip that I perfected my own approach to outlining while working on my medieval novel *Behold the Dawn*). But in the days leading up to the trip, all I could think about was the load of packing I would have to do, the stress of navigating international flights, and the time away from home.

You should know I am *not* a traveler. *Having* traveled is good. Seeing new places, breathing new air, and experiencing life through new people's eyes—that's great. The planning, though? Blech. Double blech.

But someone wise (my mother) told me the best part of a trip is looking forward to it. In other words: the planning. When I failed to enjoy the before-the-trip part of my trip, I was not only robbing myself of the joy of anticipation, I was also risking a less than smooth and splendid trip. As anyone who's been on more than two vacations knows, lack of thorough planning can sink a trip right from the start.

So it goes with a novel too.

People ask me which part of the writing process is my favorite. *Every* part is good in its own way, but, I have to admit, the outline is my favorite. The outline is where I get to *anticipate* the excitement and the new experiences I'll discover in the first draft. The outline is where I meet my story face to face—in print—for the first time. The outline is where I make sure the trip is going to be smooth sailing from start to finish.

The more thorough we are in our planning, the better our stories will be. And the more love and excitement we can lavish on our planning, the better our outlines will be.

I hope this workbook has helped you further your understanding of storytelling in general and *your* story in particular. Now that you've reached the end, it's time to grab your boarding pass and head out on that trip of a lifetime, knowing you're as well-prepared as possible. See you in the Alps!

K.M. Weiland
November 2014

Note From the Author: Thanks so much for reading! I hope you've enjoyed our exploration of outlining and have closed this workbook prepared to start a wonderful first draft. Do you know reviews sell books? If the *Outlining Your Novel Workbook* was helpful to you, would you consider rating and reviewing it on Amazon.com? Thank you and happy writing!

Want more writing tips? Join my mailing list at helpingwritersbecomeauthors.com/ outlining-your-novel-signup to receive my monthly e-letter, full of writing tips, answered questions, creativity jump-starters, inspirational quotes, updates about new books and workshops—and my free e-book *Crafting Unforgettable Characters*.

Join the discussion: #OutliningYourNovel

ACKNOWLEDGMENTS

I LOVE WRITING the acknowledgments page, because it means sitting down and thinking about all the lovely and selfless people who have spent time and energy helping me with the sometimes monumental task of creating a book. In the production of every book, there are always a handful of very specific people who had a direct influence upon the project. For this book, those people include (in no particular order):

My friends and beta readers, who astonish me with their generosity every time I ask for yet another favor:

London Crockett—who always makes me think deeper about the writing process.

Steve Mathisen—who is just about as sweet as his Pooh avatar.

Lorna G. Poston—whom I know I can always depend on for honesty and encouragement.

Liberty Speidel—who made time to read the workbook, even though she was elbow-deep in preparations for her own debut novel's launch.

Braden Russell—who always makes me think and, even better, laugh.

Ali Luke—with whom I'm honored to share this writing life.

I also have to extend a huge thank you to Chautona Havig, who sent me her brilliant spreadsheet of every single question in *Outlining Your Novel*. Also to Jim Berning, who gets all the credit for coming up with the workbook idea in the first place.

And finally, thanks, as always, to my family for their support and encouragement—and especially to my #1 fan, sister, and assistant, Amy.

ABOUT THE AUTHOR

K.M. WEILAND LIVES in make-believe worlds, talks to imaginary friends, and survives primarily on chocolate truffles and espresso. She is the IPPY and NIEA Award-winning and internationally published author of the Amazon bestsellers *Outlining Your Novel* and *Structuring Your Novel*, as well as *Jane Eyre: The Writer's Digest Annotated Classic*, the western *A Man Called Outlaw*, the medieval epic *Behold the Dawn*, and the portal fantasy *Dreamlander*. When she's not making things up, she's busy mentoring other authors through her award-winning blog HelpingWritersBecomeAuthors.com. She makes her home in western Nebraska. Visit her at KMWeiland.com or follow her on Twitter (@KMWeiland) to participate in her Writing Question of the Day (#WQOTD). You can email her at km.weiland@ymail.com.

FURTHER RESOURCES

The Negative Trait Thesaurus:
A Writer's Guide to Character Flaws
by Angela Ackerman & Becca Puglisi

Explores the possible causes, attitudes, behaviors, thoughts, and related emotions behind a character's flaws so they can be written effectively and realistically.

http://amzn.to/1oz8dF2

Write Your Novel From the Middle:
A New Approach for Plotters, Pantsers and Everyone in Between
by James Scott Bell

A truly original concept about the most important moment in your novel, the "mirror moment," and how it can be used to create unforgettable fiction.

http://amzn.to/1oXk4jX

Discover the Proven Blueprint for Creating Stories That Sell!

The *Structuring Your Novel Workbook* will show you how to:

- Implement a strong three-act structure
- Time your acts and your plot points
- Unleash your unique and personal vision for your story
- Identify common structural weaknesses and flip them into stunning strengths
- Eliminate saggy middles by discovering your story's "centerpiece"
- And so much more!

www.helpingwritersbecomeauthors.com

22907504R10081

Made in the USA
Middletown, DE
11 August 2015